Symbolic AI

The Power of Rule-Based Intelligence and Knowledge Systems

Taylor Royce

DEDICATION

To the bright minds of the past, present, and future who have the courage to investigate, challenge, and reshape the limits of artificial intelligence.

To the scientists, engineers, and intellectuals who consider that intelligence is more than patterns, that reasoning is just as important as learning, and that ethics, openness, and human values should always be the guiding principles in the development of AI.

To those who go beyond automation and see a time when people and machines work together rather than merely doing calculations.

You should read this book.

DISCLAIMER

This book is meant solely for educational and informational purposes. The content is offered "as is" with no explicit or implied warranties, despite every attempt to guarantee accuracy, completeness, and relevancy. Regarding the accuracy, applicability, and dependability of the information in this book for any particular purpose, the author and publisher offer no guarantees.

As of the time of writing, the talks on artificial intelligence, symbolic AI, and related technologies are grounded in the most recent findings and research. Since AI is a quickly developing area, subsequent advancements could change or build upon the concepts discussed here. When using AI principles in real-world or business settings, readers are advised to confirm important material from other sources and seek advice from experts in the field.

Any direct, indirect, incidental, consequential, or other damages resulting from the use or reliance on the material in this book are not the responsibility of the publisher or the author. Any mention of particular products, companies, or technologies is purely illustrative and does not imply endorsement.

Professional, financial, or legal advice is not offered in this book. For specific issues pertaining to AI ethics, implementation, or business strategy, readers should consult with experienced experts.

CONTENTS

ACKNOWLEDGMENTS

The process of writing this book involved extensive research, introspection, and close interaction with the artificial intelligence community. My sincere appreciation goes out to everyone who helped make this work possible.

Above all, I would like to express my gratitude to the academics, scientists, and intellectuals who founded symbolic artificial intelligence through their pioneering work. The development of AI technology is still influenced and inspired by their efforts.

I am also appreciative of the larger AI community, which includes scholars, developers, and practitioners, whose papers, conversations, and inventions offered priceless insights during the book's writing. Their research provides direction for comprehending the intricacies and possibilities of artificial intelligence.

I would like to express my profound gratitude to my peers, mentors, and coworkers who participated in stimulating discussions, questioned my viewpoints, and offered helpful criticism. Your support and intellectual interest have greatly enhanced this work.

I would especially like to thank my family, friends, and loved ones for their steadfast understanding, patience, and support during this journey. Their support was crucial because writing a book takes time, commitment, and concentration.

Lastly, I would like to thank all of the readers, be they researchers, students, AI enthusiasts, or professionals in the business, for their interest in this work. In your quest to comprehend symbolic artificial intelligence and its significance for the future of artificial intelligence, I hope this book proves to be a useful tool.

CHAPTER 1

Overview of Symbolic AI

Over the years, the science of artificial intelligence has experienced substantial changes. Although machine learning and neural networks are the main focus of current AI studies, much of the groundwork for these improvements was established by an earlier paradigm known as Good Old-Fashioned AI (GOFAI). To represent information and carry out reasoning tasks, GOFAI, or Symbolic AI, uses explicitly stated rules, logic, and symbols. This chapter offers a thorough overview of symbolic artificial intelligence, examining its history, underlying ideas, advantages, disadvantages, and parallels to contemporary AI methods.

1.1 GOFAI's History: The Inception of Rule-Based AI

Symbolic AI has its roots in the 1950s and 1960s, when scientists were working to create robots that could think like humans. In order to create intelligent systems, early AI researchers concentrated on formal logic, structured knowledge representation, and established rules as opposed to contemporary machine learning, which depends on vast amounts of data and statistical patterns.

Important turning points in the history of GOFAI include:

- The Dartmouth Conference (1956): Often regarded as the inception of artificial intelligence, this gathering included pioneers including Herbert Simon, Allen Newell, Marvin Minsky, and John McCarthy. They saw artificial intelligence (AI) as a field in which computers could be taught to reason and think like people.
- Early AI Programs: Scientists created tools such as the General Problem Solver (GPS) and Logic Theorist that employed symbolic reasoning to solve structured problems and prove mathematical theorems. These applications showed that computers were capable of manipulating symbols in a manner that mirrored rational human reasoning.

- The Rise of Expert Systems (1970s-1980s) According to GOFAI, expert systems AI algorithms created to emulate human expertise in particular fields were created as computer power expanded. Examples are DENDRAL, which is used for chemical analysis, and MYCIN, which is used for medical diagnosis.

At first, there was a lot of hope for GOFAI since scientists thought that machines could achieve real intelligence by encoding human knowledge into formal rules. But the intricacy of practical knowledge and reasoning quickly exposed this method's shortcomings.

1.2 Essential Ideas: Rules, Logic, and Symbolic Reasoning

The foundation of symbolic artificial intelligence is symbolic reasoning, in which AI systems process data using explicitly defined symbols and rules. This methodology is predicated on the idea that intelligence may be formally expressed using structured knowledge and logic.

Important elements of symbolic AI:

1. Representation of Knowledge and Symbols

In GOFAI, symbols stand in for actual things like things, ideas, or connections.

- A symbolic representation of a cat might be "CAT," which is associated with qualities like "HAS_FUR" and "IS_AN_ANIMAL."
- Ontologies, semantic networks, and logical statements are examples of structured formats in which knowledge is kept.

2. Logical Inference and Deductive Reasoning

Symbolic AI infers new facts from current knowledge using formal logic, such as propositional logic and first-order logic.

For instance:

- Rule of thumb: "If X is a mammal, then X has lungs."
- The truth is that "a dolphin is a mammal."
- Conclusion Inferred: "A dolphin has lungs."
- AI systems can draw conclusions methodically

thanks to this structured reasoning, which is comparable to human deductive reasoning.

3. Systems Based on Rules

GOFAI uses if-then rules to solve issues and make judgments.

For instance:

- Rule of thumb: "If a patient has a fever and a sore throat, then they might have an infection."
- The information provided is "John has a fever and a sore throat."
- As a result, "John might have an infection."

These rule-based systems serve as the foundation for expert systems that are employed in fields like finance, engineering, and medicine.

4. Search Algorithms in Symbolic AI

GOFAI frequently investigates potential solutions using search-based methods. For problem-solving, common search techniques include breadth-first search (BFS) and depth-first search (DFS).

- An algorithm for pathfinding optimization.
- In order to make structured decisions, it is necessary

to consider constraint satisfaction problems (CSPs).

1.3 Symbolic AI's Benefits and Drawbacks

Symbolic AI's advantages

1. Transparency and Explainability

Symbolic AI systems are highly interpretable because they explicitly define the decision-making process.

- For instance, a physician in an expert medical system can examine the reasoning process that led to a diagnosis.

2. Logical Consistency

- Symbolic AI guarantees consistent and repeatable reasoning because it is founded on formal rules.
- Symbolic AI does not suffer from black-box decision-making like contemporary deep learning does.

3. Rule-based artificial intelligence (AI) performs best in structured settings where knowledge can be clearly defined.

- For instance, AI for legal reasoning can examine contracts and laws using preset rules.

4. Minimal Data Dependence

- Symbolic AI may operate with explicitly coded knowledge, in contrast to machine learning, which needs large volumes of data.
- For situations where data is scarce or unreliable, this makes it helpful.

Symbolic AI's Limitations

1. Scalability Issues

- Updating and maintaining rules gets more difficult as rule-based systems expand.
- For instance, a medical expert system with thousands of rules would find it difficult to deal with newly discovered illnesses and changing medical knowledge.

2. Lack of Adaptability

- Symbolic AI needs manual rule updates to take new information into account; it does not **learn from experience.

- It is less effective in dynamic or uncertain environments because of its rigidity.

3. GOFAI finds it difficult to grasp the uncertainty, context, and common sense that are frequently a part of human thinking.

- Example: Purely rule-based AI finds it difficult to comprehend sarcasm in natural language.

4. Computational Inefficiency for Large Problems

- When working with complex problem spaces, symbolic AI systems may become computationally costly.
- For instance, brute-force search-based chess AI is much less effective than contemporary machine-learning-based methods.

1.4 GOFAI vs. Contemporary AI: Rule-Based Systems vs. Neural Networks

In many applications, symbolic AI has been essentially superseded in recent years by machine learning (ML) and neural networks. These two paradigms differ primarily in the following ways:

The following are the characteristics of symbolic artificial intelligence (GOFAI):

- Relies on explicitly specified rules and logic
- Very interpretable and transparent
- Requires manual programming and updating
- Performs well in organized environments but finds it difficult to handle complex real-world ambiguities

2. Features of Machine Learning (Modern AI)

- finds patterns in big datasets without the need for explicit rules
- Does well in circumstances that are unclear and unstructured
- often functions as a "black-box" (less explicable reasoning)
- Continually gets better with practice and adaptation

Use Cases Where Symbolic AI Still Works Well

- Expert systems in law and medicine (requiring strict logic and transparency)

- Ontologies and knowledge representation (used in semantic search engines)
- AI-powered automation for organized decision-making (rule-based chatbots, for example)

Hybrid AI Approaches: The Future

- Neuro-Symbolic AI is a recent field of study that focuses on fusing symbolic reasoning with machine learning.
- This hybrid strategy seeks to benefit from the adaptability of machine learning while leveraging the transparency of symbolic AI.

By introducing logical reasoning, organized knowledge representation, and rule-based systems, symbolic AI established the groundwork for artificial intelligence. Although machine learning has emerged as a result of GOFAI's shortcomings, it is still useful in domains that demand explainability, systematic reasoning, and formal logic.

CHAPTER 2

SYMBOLIC AI's MATHEMATICS AND LOGIC

In order to organize, process, and deduce knowledge, artificial intelligence, especially in its symbolic form, heavily depends on mathematical and logical concepts. Symbolic AI, also known as Good Old-Fashioned AI (GOFAI), functions using clearly defined rules and logical structures, in contrast to contemporary machine learning techniques that depend on statistical models and enormous volumes of data. This chapter examines the mathematical underpinnings of symbolic artificial intelligence, such as inference engines, automated theorem proving, propositional and predicate logic, and knowledge representation frameworks.

2.1 AI's Hypothetical and Predicate Logic

Symbolic AI is based on logic, which offers an organized framework for knowledge representation and reasoning. AI relies heavily on two main types of logic:

Logic of Propositions

Sentential logic, another name for propositional logic, deals with propositions, or assertions, that can be classified as true or false. It transforms basic assertions into complicated expressions by using logical connectives.

The following are the fundamental elements of propositional logic:

- Propositions: assertions that may or may not be true (e.g., "The sky is blue").
- **The following are examples of logical connectors:** Negation ($\neg$): This inverts the truth value (for example, "$\neg$P" indicates "not P").
- "And" is represented by the conjunction "$\wedge$). For example, "P $\wedge$ Q" is true if both P and Q are true.
- The symbol "or" is represented by the disjunction ($\vee$). For example, "P $\vee$ Q" is true if either P or Q is true.
- The expression "P $\rightarrow$ Q" indicates that if P is true, then Q must also be true. This is an example of a "if-then" statement.

- The expression "if and only if" is represented by the biconditional (↔). For example, "P ↔ Q" indicates that P is true if and only if Q is true.

Deduction and Truth Tables:

By enumerating every potential truth value, truth tables aid in the evaluation of logical expressions. Propositional logic is used in AI deductive reasoning to draw conclusions from premises.

First-Order Logic, or FOL, Predicate Logic

Propositional logic lacks expressiveness for sophisticated AI applications, although being helpful for simple thinking. By adding quantifiers, variables, and predicates that characterize the relationships between objects, predicate logic expands on propositional logic.

Components of predicate logic

- Predicates: functions that express an object's qualities (e.g., "isTall(John)") are components of predicate logic.
- The Universal Quantifier ($\forall$) indicates that a property is true for every element (for example,

"$\forall$x: Human(x) $\rightarrow$ Mortal(x)").

- "$\exists$x: Animal(x) $\wedge$ HasWings(x)" is an example of an existential quantifier ($\exists$), which indicates that at least one element possesses a particular characteristic.

AI Applications:

AI systems can reason about relationships, things, and abstract ideas thanks to predicate logic. It serves as the foundation for rule-based reasoning, expert systems, and knowledge representation.

2.2 Formal Verification and Automated Theorem Proving

The technique of employing algorithms to support or refute logical claims is known as Automated Theorem Proving (ATP). In artificial intelligence, ATP is essential for knowledge inference, software verification, and mathematical reasoning.

AI-Powered Automated Theorem Proving

Formal logic is used by ATP systems to assess a theorem's

logical validity. Among the most important ATP techniques are:

Resolution-Based Proving:

- Derives contradictions and verifies the validity of theorems through refutation.
- Prolog and other logic programming languages require it.

Tableaux Methods:

- Builds a tree of logical claims and methodically removes inconsistencies.
- Beneficial for AI applications that make decisions.

Natural Deduction:

- Uses inference rules like modus tollens and modus ponens to mimic human reasoning.
- Used in AI-based arguments, medical diagnosis, and legal reasoning.

Verification in Form

- Systems, especially software and hardware, are guaranteed to comply with their specified correctness properties through formal verification. It is essential in:

Software Verification: Confirming the correctness of a program's logic.

- Verifying sure circuits and processors operate as intended is known as hardware verification.
- Security Systems: Ensuring the perfect functioning of access control systems and cryptographic protocols.

Formal verification is aided by tools like Coq, Isabelle, and Z3, which enable AI systems to rigorously reason about accuracy.

2.3 Using Ontologies and Frames to Represent Knowledge

AI requires a systematic method of representing knowledge in order to reason about the world. Symbolic AI models information logically and hierarchically using ontologies and frames.

AI Ontologies

An organized collection of ideas and connections within a field is defined by an ontology. It includes:

- Objects and Classes: Hierarchical categories (e.g., "Golden Retriever" → "Dogs" → "Mammals").
- "Dogs have fur" is an example of an attribute that is associated with an entity.
- Connections between things (such as "isA," "partOf") are referred to as relations.

Ontology Applications

- Semantic Web: AI-powered web apps leverage ontologies to improve search engines.
- AI for medical diagnostics depends on ontology-based knowledge bases (Expert Systems:).
- Robotics: Robots can comprehend and classify objects with the aid of ontologies.

Frames as Knowledge Structures Using slots and fillers, frames offer an organized method of processing and storing AI knowledge.

Slots: An object's attributes (for example, "Car" → Slot: "Color").

Possible values for a slot (e.g., "Color" => "Red, Blue, Black") are known as fillers.

Chatbots and Virtual Assistants:

- Use frames to express user preferences in frame-based AI systems.
- Game AI: NPCs in games make decisions based on frames.
- Through organized data, Cognitive Computing: aids AI in comprehending real-world situations.

2.4 Inference Engines' Function in Symbolic AI

A symbolic AI system's reasoning part is called an inference engine. In order to make inferences, resolve issues, and produce thoughtful answers, it applies logical rules to knowledge bases.

Types of Inference in AI

- Forward Chaining: Makes inferences using rules after starting with known facts.

- Utilized in rule-based AI and expert systems
- For instance, by assuming that "All birds can fly" and "Sparrows are birds," one might conclude that "Sparrows can fly."

The process of "backward chaining" involves starting with an objective and working backward to gather data that support it.

- Common in AI reasoning systems and Prolog programming.
- To demonstrate that sparrows are able to fly, for instance, see whether "all birds can fly" and "sparrows are birds."

Inference Engine Applications

- Expert Systems: Inference engines are used in financial advisory AI, legal reasoning, and medical diagnosis.
- Game AI: Inference is used in strategy games to forecast the moves of their opponents.
- Natural Language Processing: AI chatbots use contextual principles to deduce meaning.

The rule-based inference engine CLIPS is a popular example of a key inference engine technology.

- Drools: A system for managing business rules.
- Prolog: An AI inference logic programming language.

Symbolic AI's logical and mathematical underpinnings offer a framework for knowledge representation, reasoning, and problem-solving. Even if deep learning and statistical models are the main focus of current AI advances, symbolic techniques are still essential in domains that need for explainability, formal verification, and organized reasoning.

Symbolic AI is still influencing intelligent systems in important fields including healthcare, finance, law, and security by utilizing propositional and predicate logic, automated theorem proving, ontologies, frames, and inference engines. To fully utilize rule-based AI systems, it is essential to comprehend these concepts.

CHAPTER 3

THE FIRST AI REVOLUTION: EXPERT SYSTEMS

One of the first and most important developments in artificial intelligence is represented by expert systems. These rule-based computers used inference processes and organized knowledge bases to mimic human decision-making in specific domains. Expert systems were heralded as the apex of artificial intelligence in the 1970s and 1980s, with uses ranging from industrial troubleshooting to medical diagnosis. But despite their initial promise, their scalability, flexibility, and knowledge acquisition constraints ultimately caused them to decline.

This chapter investigates the operation of expert systems, looks at important cases, assesses their advantages and disadvantages, and examines how machine learning has caused them to wane.

3.1 Knowledge Bases and Inference Rules in the Operation of Expert Systems

Expert systems are made to solve complicated problems in a certain field by simulating human experts. Expert systems use well specified rules and logic-based reasoning in contrast to contemporary AI systems that rely on statistical learning from large datasets.

Expert System Components

In general, expert systems are made up of three main parts:

Knowledge Base:

- The core of an expert system, comprising rules and facts pertaining to a specific field.
- "If a patient has a high fever and a sore throat, then they may have strep throat" is an example of a if-then rule that is typically used to describe knowledge.
- Human experts create the rules, and knowledge engineers encode them into the system.

The reasoning machinery that draws conclusions by applying logical principles to existing data is known as the "Inference Engine."

- employs two main methods of reasoning:
- In forward chaining, conclusions are drawn by applying rules to known facts.
- A hypothesis is the starting point for backward chaining, which verifies supporting facts by working backward.

The part that communicates with human users, gathering data and offering justifications for the system's judgments, is called the User Interface:.

- Certain systems provide explainability features, which provide an explanation for the reasoning behind a specific decision.

Decision-Making by Expert Systems

An expert system's decision-making procedure is organized as follows:

1. Data Input: In a medical diagnosis system, the user

enters information, such as symptoms.

2. Rule Matching: The inference engine looks for relevant rules in the knowledge base.

3. Inference Execution: To draw conclusions, the system uses either forward or backward chaining.

4. Output Generation: The system uses its logic to provide actions, diagnoses, or suggestions.

Expert systems work well in fields where uncertainty is low and clear rules can be established. As knowledge bases expand, rule conflicts and inconsistencies may occur, which could compromise system dependability.

3.2 Important Illustrations: XCON, DENDRAL, and MYCIN

A number of innovative expert systems demonstrated how rule-based AI may be used to solve practical issues. MYCIN, DENDRAL, and XCON were among the most prominent.

MYCIN: The Expert System for Medical Diagnosis

- MYCIN was an AI system created at Stanford University in the 1970s that was intended to identify bacterial infections and suggest antibiotic therapies.

- MYCIN's knowledge base included guidelines developed by medical professionals that enabled it to examine bacterial cultures, patient symptoms, and blood test results.

- It handled ambiguity by giving diagnostic confidence scores using certainty factors.

- MYCIN showed that AI could match or surpass human doctors in identifying infections, despite the fact that it was never used in clinical settings because of liability issues.

DENDRAL: The System for Chemical Analysis

- One of the earliest AI algorithms capable of scientific discovery was DENDRAL, which was created at Stanford University in the 1960s.

- DENDRAL, which was created for organic chemistry, examined mass spectrometry data to ascertain the molecular makeup of unidentified substances.

- As a forerunner to the use of AI in scientific inquiry, it invented automated hypothesis generation.

The Business Configuration System, or XCON

- An expert system for configuring computer hardware components, XCON (formerly known as R1) was created by Digital Equipment Corporation (DEC) in the late 1970s.
- It ensured that components were accurately integrated in accordance with customer specifications by automating the design of complicated computer systems.
- XCON demonstrated the economic viability of expert systems by reducing human errors and greatly increasing efficiency in hardware configuration. At its height, XCON saved DEC millions of dollars yearly.

These expert systems showed off AI's capabilities in specific domains, but they also brought to light important challenges, like how hard it is to increase rule-based knowledge and adjust to new information.

3.3 Expert Systems' Benefits and Drawbacks

While there were many benefits to expert systems, they also had drawbacks.

Expert Systems' Advantages

High Accuracy in Narrow Domains:
- Expert systems may perform on par with or better than human specialists in certain domains, such as chemistry or medicine.
- Consistent Decision-Making: Expert systems did not experience weariness, bias, or amnesia like people do.
- Rule-based AI offered transparent explanations for its findings, in contrast to contemporary deep learning models that frequently function as "black boxes."
- Knowledge Preservation: Organizations were able to preserve expertise even when human specialists retired or left by codifying their knowledge.

Expert Systems' Drawbacks

- The creation and upkeep of rule-based knowledge bases necessitated substantial input from human specialists and took a lot of time. This was known as the "Knowledge Acquisition Bottleneck."
- Scalability The management of thousands of rules caused conflicts, inconsistencies, and sluggish performance as knowledge bases grew.
- Lack of Adaptability: Expert systems could not learn from new data; in order to include new information, they needed to be updated manually.
- Difficulty Handling Uncertainty: Expert systems have trouble handling unclear or insufficient data, in contrast to contemporary probabilistic AI models.

Expert systems eventually declined as a result of these constraints, and machine learning-based AI approaches emerged.

3.4 Expert Systems' Decline and Machine Learning's Ascent

Expert systems started to lose their hegemony by the late 1980s and early 1990s for a number of important reasons.

The Reasons Expert Systems Rejected

- Knowledge Engineering Bottleneck: As domains became more complex, the manual labor needed to encode expert knowledge became unfeasible.
- Lack of Generalization: Knowledge transfer between domains was difficult for rule-based systems.
- Computational Inefficiency: The cost of computing grew when searching big rule sets, resulting in sluggish reaction times.
- The late 1980s saw funding cuts for AI research due to overhyped expectations, which slowed future advancement. This is known as "The AI Winter."

The Machine Learning Transition

The emergence of machine learning (ML), which provided a data-driven approach to AI, paralleled the fall of expert systems. ML models might learn patterns from data, adjust to new information, and get better over time in place of manually encoding rules.

- AI was able to identify patterns in complicated datasets thanks to neural networks, which were inspired by the human brain.
- The inflexibility of rule-based systems was overcome by the introduction of probabilistic reasoning" by Bayesian networks, decision trees, and support vector machines.
- Big Data Revolution: The proliferation of digital data made it possible for AI systems to learn on large datasets, increasing their accuracy in tasks like predictive analytics, picture recognition, and natural language processing.

Expert systems are still helpful in highly structured sectors like banking, medical diagnostics, and legal analysis, but contemporary AI methods have essentially eclipsed its function.

The first AI revolution was ushered in by expert systems, which showed that robots could imitate expert-level decision-making via logical inference and organized knowledge. They established the foundation for domain-specific automation, explainable AI, and rule-based reasoning.

Their demise was caused by their drawbacks, though, including the knowledge acquisition bottleneck, lack of adaptation, and computational inefficiency. The paradigm changed from hand-crafted rules to statistical learning with the advent of machine learning and data-driven AI.

Expert systems continue to play a crucial role in the history of artificial intelligence, even though their use has waned. They have influenced the development of contemporary knowledge-based systems and hybrid AI techniques that combine machine learning and symbolic reasoning.

CHAPTER 4

REASONING AND KNOWLEDGE REPRESENTATION

Artificial intelligence is based on knowledge representation and reasoning (KR&R), which allows robots to process, store, and infer knowledge in an organized way. The representation of knowledge has a direct impact on an AI system's comprehension, reasoning, and decision-making capabilities. Knowledge representation in AI involves more than just storing facts; it also involves arranging data to support problem-solving, logical reasoning, and inference.

Semantic networks, frames, scripts, ontologies, taxonomies, and description logics are among the main techniques of knowledge representation that are examined in this chapter. Every technique has a unique function in organizing knowledge, assisting with thought processes, and empowering AI systems to carry out clever tasks.

4.1 Semantic Networks: Using Graphs to Represent Knowledge

Semantic networks, which use graph structures to model interactions between concepts, are a key method to knowledge representation. The entities in these networks are represented by nodes, and the relationships between them are represented by edges.

Semantic networks' salient characteristics

- Graph-Based Structure: Knowledge is shown as a network of linked nodes (relationships) and interconnected nodes (concepts).
- Hierarchical Relationships: AI systems are able to use inheritance-based reasoning when concepts are arranged in a hierarchy.
- Adaptable and Intuitive Representation: Semantic networks structurally and graphically mimic how people link ideas.

A Semantic Network Example

Take a look at this straightforward knowledge representation:

"A dog has fur"
"Dogs can bark"
"A dog is a mammal"

This knowledge is expressed as follows in a semantic network:

- "Dog" (Node) → "is-a" (Edge) → "Mammal" (Node)
- "Dog" (Node) → "has" (Edge) → "Fur" (Node)
- "Dog" (Node) → "can" (Edge) → "Bark" (Node)

AI systems can infer more facts from preexisting associations thanks to semantic networks. For example, the system can use transitive inference to determine that dogs are also warm-blooded if mammals are warm-blooded.

Semantic Network Applications

- Natural Language Processing (NLP): Used in text

comprehension, question answering, and word meaning disambiguation.

- Expert Systems: Assists AI in reasoning about hierarchical knowledge in fields such as law and medicine.
- AI is able to comprehend semantic linkages between search queries and documents" thanks to search engines and recommendation systems.

When scaled to large knowledge bases, semantic networks can become computationally complex despite their benefits, necessitating efficient retrieval and storing procedures.

4.2 Using Scripts and Frames to Structure Knowledge for AI

AI systems can store, retrieve, and manipulate knowledge efficiently with the use of frames and scripts, which are structured approaches to knowledge representation.

Structured Knowledge Units as Frames

A data structure that represents stereotypical information about things, ideas, or circumstances is called a frame. Because each frame has slots (attributes) and fillers (values), it is possible to store knowledge in an ordered manner.

For instance, a car frame

Slot	Filler
Type	Vehicle
Model	Tesla Model S
Fuel Type	Electric
Wheels	4

Frame-Based Reasoning:

- All vehicles have wheels, however certain vehicle types may override this. This is an example of inheritance made possible by frames.
- By assuming common characteristics, AI can fill in missing information (e.g., if a car type is unspecified, it assumes four wheels).

Scripts: Displaying Sequences of Events

- Scripts are useful for AI systems that need contextual knowledge because they capture typical sequences of actions in frequent scenarios and represent sequential occurrences in a structured fashion.

For instance, a restaurant dining script

1. Go into the eatery.
2. Locate a table or bide your time till seated.
3. Order meals after reading the menu.
4. Consume the meal.
5. Make the payment.
6. Get out of the eatery.

AI can predict actions and reason about occurrences thanks to scripts. A virtual assistant with a restaurant script, for instance, can recognize when to request payment details or recommend menu items.

Frame and Script Applications

- Chatbots and Virtual Assistants: Assist AI in understanding user intents and responding with contextually relevant information.
- Autonomous Vehicles: AI systems utilize frame-based knowledge to recognize road signs, vehicles, and pedestrians.
- Robotics: Used in AI-controlled robots to predict human actions and interact intelligently.

Despite their strength, frames and scripts are ill-suited to handling uncertain or partial information, which restricts their use in dynamic contexts.

4.3 Taxonomy and Ontologies: Putting Knowledge in Order for Intelligent Systems

Domain-specific knowledge in AI systems can be arranged using structured frameworks provided by ontologies and taxonomies.

Taxonomies: Concepts Classified Hierarchically

Concepts are arranged in categories and subcategories in a

taxonomy, which resembles a tree. It makes it possible for general entities to inherit properties from specialized entities.

An Animal Taxonomy as an Example

Animal:

mammal: "dog," "cat,"

bird: "eagle," and "sparrow."

Although taxonomies aid AI systems in effectively classifying and retrieving information, they are not flexible enough to depict complex relationships beyond parent-child structures.

Ontologies: Complex Representation of Knowledge

By defining concepts, relationships, and rules inside a certain domain, an ontology expands taxonomies. AI can think about relationships outside of hierarchical systems thanks to ontologies.

Medical Ontology, for instance

Disease:

- Accompanying symptoms
- Treatable with

Drug:

- It is recommended for
- Has adverse effects

Ontologies in AI Applications

Assisting AI in reasoning about symptom-disease relationships

Medical Diagnosis Systems:

- Semantic Web: Allows search engines to understand the meaning behind web content.
- Legal AI Systems: Provide legal reasoning by representing laws, rules, and case precedents.

The development of ontologies necessitates significant human expertise and domain-specific knowledge, yet they offer rich, organized representations of knowledge.

4.4 Description Logics' Function in Knowledge Graphs

Ontologies and knowledge graphs are formally based on description logics (DL). They make it possible for artificial intelligence systems to apply logical reasoning to organized data.

Description Logics' salient characteristics

- Formal Semantics: Gives concepts, roles, and relationships exact meaning.
- AI is able to infer new facts from preexisting information thanks to automated reasoning.
- The ability to classify new items using pre-existing descriptions is made possible by concept inference.

Description Logic Reasoning Example

- "All mammals are warm-blooded."
- "Dogs are mammals."
- The conclusion is that "dogs are warm-blooded."

AI Applications

- Google's Knowledge Graph, IBM Watson, and biomedical AI all use knowledge graphs.
- Automated Decision Support: Assists AI systems in validating and inferring novel relationships in complex datasets.

When used on large-scale knowledge bases, description logics can be computationally costly notwithstanding their strength. Probabilistic reasoning is one optimization technique that can lessen these difficulties.

AI's ability to understand, organize, and infer knowledge" is based on knowledge representation and reasoning. A variety of techniques, such as semantic networks, frames, scripts, ontologies, and description logics play essential roles in structuring AI systems' perception of the world.

These approaches have disadvantages even though they offer organized reasoning capabilities. AI systems can now reason logically while adapting to new data thanks to hybrid techniques that combine rule-based reasoning with statistical inference brought about by the rise of **machine learning-based AI.

CHAPTER 5

APPLICATIONS OF RULE-BASED SYSTEMS

Since the inception of artificial intelligence (AI), rule-based systems have been fundamental to the field. These systems rely on if-then rules to process information, make decisions, and infer new knowledge. In contrast to contemporary AI methods that depend on extensive data-driven learning, rule-based systems offer explicit reasoning paths, which makes them extremely interpretable and dependable in fields that demand transparency.

The fundamental ideas of rule-based systems are examined in this chapter, including logical programming, business rule management systems (BRMS), and production systems. Additionally, it explores real-world applications of symbolic AI in finance, law, and healthcare, among other areas.

5.1 Production Systems: Symbolic AI at its Core: Rules

Rule-based AI is built on a production system, which uses a set of production rules to decide what to do depending on facts. The condition-action (if-then) structure of these rules facilitates logical reasoning and decision-making.

A Production System's Components

- A set of if-then rules that specify system behavior are stored in the Knowledge Base (Rule Base).
- As an illustration, diagnose a patient with the flu if they have a fever and a sore throat.

- The system's current state of facts is stored in the Working Memory (Fact Base).
- As rules are applied, facts are changed, enabling dynamic reasoning.

Inference Engine
- Regulates the application and execution of rules.
- Employs two primary methods of reasoning:
- Forward Chaining: Using rules, new facts are

inferred from known facts.

- Backward Chaining: locates supporting evidence by working backward from a goal.

When more than one rule fits the facts at hand, the Conflict Resolution Mechanism decides which rule should be repealed.

Among the tactics are:

- Specificity: More specific regulations take precedence over general ones.
- The preference is for rules that are prompted by more recent facts.

Rule-Based Medical Diagnosis as an Example

Rules like these could be part of a production system for diagnosing common illnesses:

- A respiratory infection should be taken into consideration if a patient has a fever and cough.
- A meningitis test should be performed then if a patient has a high temperature and a strong headache.

Rule-based systems are ideal for crucial decision-making activities because of the transparency and consistency guaranteed by this structured reasoning method.

Production Systems' Benefits and Drawbacks

Benefits:

- Explainability: AI judgments can be linked to rules, boosting system confidence.
- Reliability: Consistent decision-making without reliance on data is provided by rules.
- In contrast to machine learning models, adding or changing rules does not necessitate retraining.

Disadvantages:

- Difficulties with Scalability: Overseeing thousands of rules gets difficult.
- Managing Uncertainty: Conventional rule-based systems have trouble processing unclear or insufficient data.
- Performance Constraints: Inference may be slowed down by searching huge rule sets.

To get around these restrictions, contemporary AI systems frequently mix rule-based reasoning with probabilistic techniques.

5.2 Industry Use of Business Rule Management Systems (BRMS)

Business Rule Management Systems (BRMS) offer automated decision-making frameworks to businesses, separating application code from business logic. This eliminates the need for in-depth programming knowledge and enables non-technical professionals to develop and oversee policies.

Key Features of BRMS

- Rule Authoring and Editing: Without programming, business analysts are able to create and edit rules.
- Decision Automation: To optimize operations, BRMS implements rules in real-time.
- Business application integration: Complements workflow, CRM, and ERP systems.

BRMS Application Cases in Industry

1. Banking and Finance

- Fraud Detection: BRMS uses pre-established risk rules to identify suspicious transactions.
- To approve or deny loans, Loan Approval: considers income, debt-to-income ratio, and credit ratings.

2. Healthcare

- Medical Insurance Processing: based on policy rules, automatically ascertains claim eligibility.
- Based on medical guidelines, clinical decision support offers doctors treatment recommendations.

3. Retail and E-commerce

- Dynamic Pricing: Modifies product prices in response to competition prices, seasonality, and demand.
- Customer Segmentation: Tailors marketing tactics according to consumer purchasing patterns.

BRMS Advantages and Difficulties

Advantages:

- Agility: By revising regulations, businesses can promptly adjust to regulatory changes.
- Consistency guarantees consistent decision-making throughout an organization.
- Improved Compliance: By enforcing established guidelines, it helps comply with industry and regulatory laws.

Challenges

- It can be difficult to manage thousands of interconnected rules. This is one of the challenges.
- Initial Implementation Costs: A large investment is needed to set up an enterprise-grade BRMS.

Notwithstanding these difficulties, BRMS is essential to automating decision-making in a variety of sectors, lowering human error and enhancing operational effectiveness.

5.3 Prolog and Other Declarative Languages for Logical Programming

In contrast to procedural code, logical programming is a declarative paradigm that expresses information in terms of logic propositions. It offers a strong basis for AI logic and problem-solving.

The Foundation of Logical AI: Prolog

The most popular logic programming language is called Prolog (Programming in Logic). Inferring conclusions by backward chaining, it works with facts, rules, and queries.

The Prolog Knowledge Base for Family Relationships is an example.

```
parent(john, mary).
parent(mary, susan).

ancestor(X, Y) :- parent(X, Y).
ancestor(X, Y) :- parent(X, Z), ancestor(Z, Y).
```

Explanation:

- The system is aware that Mary is Susan's parent and John is Mary's.
- According to the rule, an ancestor is either a parent or a parent of an ancestor.
- Since John is Susan's grandpa, a query such as ancestor(john, susan). would yield true.

Logical Programming Applications

- Utilized in medical diagnosis, legal reasoning, and troubleshooting
- Expert Systems: Natural Language Processing (NLP): Aids in the parsing and comprehension of sentence structures.
- Automated Planning: AI systems create action sequences through logical programming.

While logical programming has powerful inferencing capabilities, it is not well-suited for processing large-scale, unstructured data, which has led to the growth of machine learning-based AI techniques.

5.4 Case Studies: Finance, Law, and Healthcare Using Symbolic AI

1. One of the first rule-based expert systems for identifying bacterial infections and suggesting antibiotics was MYCIN (1970s).

- Modern Clinical Decision Support Systems (CDSS): Rule-based AI is used by hospitals to help physicians diagnose conditions and recommend treatments.

2. Law: Automatic Legal Reasoning

- Legal Expert Systems: AI generates case law recommendations.
- Contract Analysis: Rule-based AI extracts key terms and compliance requirements from legal documents by analyzing statutes and legal precedents.

3. Finance: Fraud Detection and Risk Assessment

- Regulatory Compliance: Assures that financial institutions adhere to laws such as Anti-Money Laundering (AML) regulations.

- Rule-Based Fraud Detection: identifies suspicious transactions based on predefined fraud patterns.

The persistent applicability of rule-based AI in structured, high-stakes decision-making contexts are demonstrated by these case studies.

Even though machine learning is the main focus of current AI research, rule-based AI systems are still essential in symbolic reasoning and automated decision-making. In regulated industries, symbolic AI offers explainability, reliability, and compliance advantages.

The next generation of intelligent decision systems will be driven by hybrid approaches that combine rule-based reasoning with probabilistic learning as AI develops further.

CHAPTER 6

USING SYMBOLIC AI FOR NATURAL LANGUAGE PROCESSING

A crucial area of artificial intelligence is natural language processing (NLP), which gives robots the ability to comprehend, interpret, and produce human language. While deep learning and statistical techniques are major components of modern NLP, symbolic AI was essential to the early development of NLP. Symbolic techniques are very interpretable since they are based on explicit rules, logical reasoning, and organized representations of language.

The historical foundations of natural language processing (NLP) in symbolic AI are examined in this chapter. Early systems such as ELIZA and SHRDLU are covered, along with grammar-based parsing, ontologies, and hybrid approaches that combine machine learning and symbolic reasoning.

6.1 ELIZA, SHRDLU, and LUNAR: Early NLP Systems

Rule-based and symbolic AI approaches that processed human language using manually created linguistic rules dominated the early days of natural language processing. These groundbreaking techniques laid the groundwork for modern NLP advancements and offered insightful information on language comprehension.

The First Chatbot: ELIZA (1966)

ELIZA, one of the earliest programs to mimic human-like speech, was created by Joseph Weizenbaum at MIT. It engaged people in conversation by using a pattern-matching and substitution approach.

- In order to answer, ELIZA looked for keywords in user input and used pre-made templates.
- By rewording user words into questions to promote interaction, it imitated a Rogerian psychotherapist.

For instance:

- User: I'm depressed today.
- ELIZA: What's causing your sadness today?

ELIZA's limitations:

- No real comprehension: ELIZA just rearranged words and failed to grasp meaning.
- Strict answers: ELIZA was unable to provide a meaningful response if a user's input did not follow predetermined patterns.

Notwithstanding its drawbacks, ELIZA showed the potential of NLP and stimulated more conversational AI research.

SHRDLU: Interpreting Language in a Constrained World (1971)

SHRDLU was a revolutionary natural language processing system created by Terry Winograd at MIT that was able to understand and control objects in a block-based virtual environment.

To interpret user commands, SHRDLU employed symbolic

reasoning and structured grammar.

For instance:

- User: Take up the red block.
- SHRDLU: (Shifts the red block forward)
- The system was able to process complex commands such as these because it kept a knowledge base about objects, colors, and spatial relationships.
- The red brick should be stacked on top of the blue block.

SHRDLU's Strengths:

- Intense language comprehension in a supervised setting. The system was able to infer implicit information using logical reasoning.

SHRDLU's limitations:

- Narrow scope: Could only operate in its **simplified universe of blocks.
- Lack of adaptation in the real world: Incapable of processing human language that is open-ended.

SHRDLU illustrated the challenge of scaling rule-based systems to practical applications while proving that symbolic AI may be utilized for structured language understanding.

Domain-Specific Natural Language Processing for Science (LUNAR, 1973)

LUNAR was created by William Woods to process natural language queries pertaining to lunar rock samples that were gathered during the Apollo missions.

To comprehend scientific issues, it made use of a symbolic parsing engine and a sizable collection of structured facts.

- Examples of queries that LUNAR could process:
- "What is the titanium content of sample 10017?"
- "Which samples contain both olivine and plagioclase?"

LUNAR's contributions:

- Disseminated the use of structured knowledge bases for information retrieval.
- Proved that rule-based NLP could handle specialized scientific areas.

But just like SHRDLU, LUNAR has trouble with ambiguous wording and open-ended questions.

6.2 Symbolic Methods for Grammar and Parsing Analysis

The capacity of symbolic AI in NLP to assess grammar, syntax, and sentence structure is one of its main advantages. To analyze sentences and derive meaning, symbolic techniques rely on explicit rules and formal language theories.

Important Techniques for Symbolic Parsing

One example of a set of rules for organizing sentences" is provided by Context-Free Grammars (CFGs).

- Sentence → Noun Phrase + Verb Phrase
- Noun Phrase → Article + Noun
- Verb Phrase → Verb + Noun Phrase

Provides systematic sentence parsing according to preset rules.

Sentence structures are represented by finite state machines in Augmented Transition Networks (ATNs).

- Capable of handling complex language phenomena and more adaptable than CFGs

In contrast to phrase structures, Dependency Parsing examines word dependencies.

- The line "The dog chased the cat," is an example.
- "Chased" serves as the primary verb.
- "Dog" is the subject, and it is associated with "chased."
- "Cat" is the object, and it is also associated with "chased."

Symbolic Parsing Benefits:

- Offers explainability in language comprehension.
- Effectively manages formal and structured text.

Difficulties:

- Strict rules have trouble with informal and unclear language.
- Hard to scale for varied linguistic variations.

6.3 Ontologies' Function in Semantic Interpretation

A domain's concepts, connections, and categories are defined by an ontology, which is an organized representation of knowledge. By offering contextual meaning beyond syntactic parsing, ontologies improve natural language processing.

Important Ontology Elements:
- Concepts: Denote entities such as "Car," "Person," and "Disease."
- Connections: Describe the connections between ideas (e.g., "Doctor treats Patient").
- Sort ideas into more general or more specialized terms using hierarchies (e.g., "Mammal" → "Dog").

Ontology Applications in NLP:

- By comprehending human intent, semantic search enhances search engines.
- Medical NLP: Aids in the processing of clinical records and the identification of illnesses, symptoms,

and therapies.

- Chatbots: By offering structured information, they improve conversational AI.

By bridging the gap between syntax and semantics, ontologies enable symbolic AI systems to understand the meaning behind words.

6.4 Hybrid AI: Blending Statistical and Symbolic Natural Language Processing

In order to improve performance, modern NLP is progressively integrating symbolic AI with machine learning approaches.

Why Use Hybrid AI?

- Structure and explainability are provided via symbolic AI.
- Statistical techniques, such as deep learning, deal with variation and ambiguity.
- Accuracy and transparency are maintained when both are combined.

Tips for Hybrid NLP:

1. Machine Learning + Grammar-Based Parsing

- The structure is based on symbolic syntax rules.
- Uses machine learning models to handle informal language and exceptions.

2. Ontology-Guided Deep Learning

- Deep learning models learn representations using structured knowledge.
- Symbolic ontologies assist structure unstructured text data.

3. Rule-Based Chatbots with Neural Response Generation

- Rule-based AI responds to particular inquiries.
- Neural networks produce answers in the event that preset rules are not met.

The development of context-aware chatbots, intelligent search engines, and AI-driven assistants that integrate logical reasoning with statistical learning is being made possible by hybrid AI, which is propelling advancements in natural language processing.

By offering structured language processing techniques through early chatbots, grammar parsing, and ontologies, symbolic AI has contributed significantly to natural language processing (NLP). The future of language technology is being shaped by hybrid AI systems that combine logical reasoning with machine learning, even if statistical natural language processing has outperformed solely symbolic methods.

NLP is becoming increasingly accurate, explainable, and adaptable to real-world applications by combining the advantages of both paradigms.

CHAPTER 7

SYMBOLIC AI AND KNOWLEDGE GRAPHS IN THE CONTEMPORARY ERA

A potent technique for arranging, categorizing, and making use of enormous volumes of data is the knowledge graph. They give AI systems the ability to reason, draw novel conclusions, and offer more contextually relevant insights by representing relationships between things in a structured, machine-readable format. Knowledge graphs provide semantic understanding in contrast to traditional databases, which makes them an essential part of symbolic AI in the contemporary day.

The structure and components of knowledge graphs, their practical uses, methods for creating and managing large-scale graphs, and how they are developing to interact with deep learning and neural networks for more advanced AI capabilities are all covered in detail in this chapter.

7.1 Knowledge Graphs: What Are They? Components and Structure

A data structure that connects items through relationships in a network-like fashion is called a knowledge graph (KG). Knowledge graphs employ a graph-based model in which data is represented as nodes and edges, in contrast to relational databases, which store data in tables.

A Knowledge Graph's Essential Elements

1. Entities (Nodes):

- Depict concepts, abstract ideas, or actual objects.

For instance:

- An individual ("Alan Turing")
- A business ("Google")
- An idea from science ("Quantum Computing")

2. Relationships (Edges): describe the connections between entities.

Examples include

- "Google → acquired → DeepMind" and "Alan

Turing → invented → Turing Machine."

3. Attributes (Properties): Entity-specific information. **For instance:**

- A person's birthdate, nationality, and occupation
- A product's cost, producer, and details

4. Ontology (Schema): describes the kinds of entities and relationships that are permitted in the graph.

- Enables reasoning and guarantees data consistency.

5. Inference Engine: Infers new facts by using symbolic reasoning.

- In the event where "Einstein was a physicist" and "Physicists study physics," for instance, the graph infers that "Einstein studied physics."

Knowledge graphs allow machines to comprehend language, answer questions, and support decision-making in a more human-like manner by structuring information in this way.

7.2 Knowledge Graph Applications: IBM Watson, Google, and Others

Large corporations currently use knowledge graphs as an essential component of AI systems. Search engines, chatbots, recommendation systems, and enterprise AI solutions are powered by them.

1. The first is the Google Knowledge Graph.

- In order to improve search results by understanding the links between entities, Google launched the Knowledge Graph in 2012.

It assists in disambiguating queries by identifying words with several meanings.

- For instance, searching for "Jaguar" could result in results for a football team, a vehicle brand, or an animal. Depending on the search context, the knowledge graph resolves this ambiguity.

Rich, organized search results are provided.

- For instance, a search for "Marie Curie" yields more than simply online links; it also yields a summary, achievements, and connected people.

- Enables natural question-answering, which enhances voice assistants (Google Assistant, Siri).

2. IBM Watson

Knowledge graphs are used by IBM Watson in a number of sectors, such as healthcare, finance, and customer service.

Watson helps physicians in healthcare by:

- Examining patient records and medical literature.
- Based on knowledge graphs of diseases, symptoms, and medications, recommendations are made for diagnosis and treatment options.

By connecting entities such as accounts, users, and transactions to uncover hidden patterns, Watson assists in the detection of fraudulent transactions in the finance industry.

3. Facebook (Meta) Social Graph

Users, pages, and interactions are represented by Facebook's Social Graph.

- Utilized for targeted advertising, content ranking,

and friend recommendations.

- Through interaction-based preference prediction, personalized news feeds are made possible.

4. Product Knowledge Graph on Amazon

- Knowledge graphs are used by Amazon to: Improve product recommendations by tying products to user behavior.
- Enhance search results by knowing user intent, categories, and synonyms.

These examples show how knowledge graphs allow intelligent decision-making in contemporary AI systems and structure huge data.

7.3 Creating and Managing Knowledge Graphs on a Large Scale

It takes data collection, integration, validation, and ongoing updates to build a large-scale knowledge graph.

1. Knowledge Graph Data Sources

Data is gathered to fill a knowledge graph from:

- Structured databases, such as Wikidata, Freebase, and Wikipedia
- Unstructured text (such as novels, research papers, and news items)
- Content created by users (such as reviews, social media, and forum posts)

2. Knowledge Graph Construction Techniques

- Experts handcraft relationships and ontologies.
- Manual Curation: It guarantees high accuracy but does not scale well.

Automated Information Extraction:

- This method extracts facts from text using Natural Language Processing (NLP) and machine learning.
- As an illustration, a system analyzes scientific papers and derives associations such as "COVID-19 $\rightarrow$ affects $\rightarrow$ Lungs"."

Crowdsourcing:

- Users can add facts to platforms such as Wikidata.
- Diverse input is ensured, but fact-checking

mechanisms are needed.

3. Keeping a Knowledge Graph Current

Consistent Updates:

- There needs to be added new knowledge (e.g., new scientific findings).
- It is necessary to remove or correct any outdated or inaccurate information.

Error Handling:

- It is necessary to resolve conflicting data, such as two distinct birthdates for the same individual.
- Prioritizes trustworthy sources using trust scores.

The efficient handling of massive knowledge graphs is facilitated by distributed storage and graph databases (e.g., Neo4j, Amazon Neptune).

Maintaining and creating knowledge graphs is a continuous challenge that calls for striking a balance between completeness, accuracy, and computational efficiency.

7.4 Knowledge Graphs' Future: Combining Deep Learning

Knowledge graphs are being combined with deep learning as AI develops to build more intelligent and flexible systems.

1. Knowledge Graph Embeddings

- Creates vector representations from knowledge graph entities and relationships.
- Enables neural networks to process graph information efficiently.
- Used in recommendation systems and semantic search engines.

2. Neural-Symbolic AI

- Combines symbolic reasoning (knowledge graphs) with neural networks.
- Example: A medical AI can: Use deep learning to spot symptoms in medical photos.
- Use a knowledge graph to reason about diseases and treatments.

3. Knowledge graphs that update themselves

- AI programs are capable of autonomously extracting new knowledge from databases, movies, and text.
- Maintains knowledge graphs current and dynamic.

4. Personalized AI Assistants

New assistants (Alexa, Google Assistant) will:

- Comprehend intricate connections between user interests, preferences, and previous interactions.
- Make shrewd, context-aware recommendations.

Combining deep learning with symbolic AI is converting knowledge graphs into self-improving, reasoning-based systems that improve AI's capacity to comprehend and engage with the world.

One of the most advanced developments in symbolic AI is represented by knowledge graphs, which provide an organized method of modeling entities, relationships, and contextual information. Knowledge graphs are influencing the direction of AI applications, from enabling Google Search to improving medical AI.

The combination of deep learning, natural language processing, and knowledge graphs will allow robots to think, reason, and adapt more like humans as we progress toward hybrid AI systems. AI understands and interacts with knowledge in a fundamentally more human way in the future, as the era of self-updating, intelligent knowledge graphs is just getting started.

CHAPTER 8

SYMBOLIC AI, PLANNING, AND DECISION MAKING

The desire to efficiently plan, make judgments, and carry out tasks has long motivated artificial intelligence. Symbolic AI is essential in these fields because of its capacity to represent knowledge and reason logically. This chapter explores the frameworks and techniques that enable AI systems to plan, optimize, and adapt, from traditional AI planning models to contemporary robotics applications.

8.1 Traditional AI Scheduling: State Space Search and STRIPS

In AI, planning is the process of creating a series of steps to accomplish a particular objective. It entails looking through potential courses of action and states in order to identify the best or most practical one. Planning in classical AI is based on well-defined formal models like state-space search and STRIPS (Stanford Research Institute Problem Solver).

STRIPS (Problem Solver from Stanford Research Institute)

STRIPS, which was created in the early 1970s, offered an organized method for defining planning issues in terms of:

- Initial State: The system's initial conditions.
- The intended result or collection of circumstances that the AI should accomplish is known as the "Goal State."
- Operators (Actions): Described in terms of postconditions (effects that follow the action) and preconditions (requirements that must be true for the action to occur).

In order to investigate various action sequences that change the original state into the desired state, STRIPS uses search methods. This approach laid the groundwork for AI planning and impacted subsequent systems.

Search in State Space

A broad strategy for AI planning is state space search, which entails investigating every potential state and its transitions. Important techniques consist of:

- Before going deeper, the Breadth-First Search (BFS): investigates every action that could be taken at each level. If the cost of each action is the same, an ideal solution is guaranteed.
- Depth-First Search (DFS): completely investigates a single path before turning around. memory-efficient, but prone to become trapped in lengthy or deep pathways.
- A Search: Balances exploration and cost estimation by employing heuristics to effectively direct the search toward the objective.

With uses in anything from robotics to gaming AI, state space search is still a key idea in AI.

8.2 Optimization and Constraint Satisfaction Issues

Constraints are requirements that must be met for a solution to be considered valid in many real-world AI planning and decision-making situations. AI systems can overcome these constraints with the use of optimization techniques and Constraint Satisfaction Problems (CSPs).

Issues with Constraint Satisfaction (CSPs)

A CSP includes:

- The items that will be given values are known as variables.
- The range of values that any variable can have is known as its domain.
- Restrictions: Guidelines that specify appropriate correlations between variables.

For instance, Sudoku puzzles and scheduling issues (such as allocating exam times without conflicts) can be formulated as CSPs. To solve these issues, one must:

- A brute-force search that repeatedly assigns values and removes erroneous ones is known as "backtracking."
- Forward Checking: Reduces the search space by removing impossible values early.

- Utilizing inference techniques, constraint propagation eliminates superfluous alternatives and infers valid assignments.

AI Planning Optimization

Beyond CSPs, optimization also applies to situations involving decision-making with several goals. Among the methods are:

- Planning logistics and allocating resources are two applications of linear programming.
- Genetic Algorithms: These algorithms use mutation and selection to solve difficult decision-making issues, drawing inspiration from natural evolution.
- Simulated Annealing: A probabilistic technique that permits sporadic upward movements in the search space, hence assisting in avoiding local optima.

Modern AI applications in banking, logistics, and automated decision-making are powered by CSPs and optimization algorithms.

8.3 Symbolic Decision Systems and Case-Based Reasoning

While conventional AI planning and optimization methods depend on explicit rules and logic, Case-Based Reasoning (CBR) is an alternative method that draws lessons from prior events.

CBR stands for "Case-Based Reasoning."
CBR is an AI decision-making approach that solves new problems by referring to similar historical occurrences. It follows a cycle of:

1. Retrieval: Identifying past cases that resemble the current problem.
2. Adaptation: Changing the previous solution to accommodate the new circumstance.
3. Evaluation: Verifying the validity of the modified solution.
4. Learning: Preserving the recently resolved case for later use.

A medical artificial intelligence system that uses CBR, for

instance, might diagnose a patient by comparing their symptoms to those of prior instances and modifying therapy suggestions appropriately.

Systems of Symbolic Decision Making

Structured, rule-based decision-making is made possible by symbolic AI through:

- Rule-based AI models that simulate human decision-making are known as "expert systems" (e.g., MYCIN for medical diagnosis).
- Logic-based decision trees are hierarchical structures in which a decision criterion is represented by each node.
- Production Systems: Systems that iteratively enhance solutions using condition-action principles.

Legal reasoning, automated troubleshooting, and medical diagnosis all make extensive use of CBR and symbolic decision systems.

8.4 Robotics Using Symbolic AI: Planning and Performing Tasks

Complex planning and decision-making skills are necessary for robotics. Symbolic AI plays a significant role in task planning, enabling robots to execute complex sequences of tasks efficiently.

Robotics Task Planning

In dynamic circumstances, robots must decide how to accomplish objectives. This is made possible by symbolic AI through:

- High-level activities can be divided into smaller subtasks using Hierarchical Task Networks (HTNs).
- Goal Regression: Determining the necessary steps by working backward from the intended outcome.
- A search and Rapidly-exploring Random Trees are two examples of motion planning algorithms that compute safe and effective movement paths.

For example, a hospital robotic assistance may use HTNs to schedule patient food deliveries, figuring out the optimal course of action depending on location and urgency limitations.

Application and Execution

A robot must carry out its strategy while making adjustments for unanticipated circumstances. Important techniques consist of:

- Sensor-Based Feedback Loops: Modifying movements based on real-time data.
- Symbolic planning and machine learning are combined in Reinforcement Learning Integration: to gradually enhance decision-making.
- Multi-Agent Coordination: Coordinating several robots or artificial intelligence agents to carry out cooperative tasks.

Symbolic AI's contribution to robotics keeps growing, bridging the gap between structured reasoning and practical adaptability.

Artificial intelligence's capacity to operate in complicated situations is based on planning, decision-making, and optimization. Symbolic AI is still crucial for directing intelligent systems, from traditional techniques like STRIPS and state space search to contemporary robotics applications. AI keeps developing by fusing learning strategies with logic-based approaches, allowing for more intelligent, dependable, and effective decision-making in a variety of fields.

CHAPTER 9

COMBINING SYMBOLIC AND SUBSYMBOLIC METHODS IN HYBRID AI

The development of artificial intelligence has been divided into two main paradigms:

subsymbolic AI, which includes methods like neural networks that learn from data, and symbolic AI, which depends on explicit rules and logic. Both strategies have proven to have advantages, but they also have drawbacks. The goal of Hybrid AI, also referred to as neuro-symbolic AI, is to integrate these techniques to produce AI systems that are more potent, flexible, and explicable.

The motivations behind hybrid AI, its technical foundations, practical applications, and the difficulties this developing field faces are all covered in this chapter.

9.1 The Hybrid AI Argument: Why Merge Neural and Symbolic Approaches?

The shortcomings of both symbolic and subsymbolic AI when applied separately serve as the driving force behind hybrid AI.

Symbolic AI's Drawbacks

Because symbolic AI follows clear guidelines and logical frameworks, it:

- Interpretable and Explainable: Users can comprehend and alter decision-making processes because knowledge is explicitly encoded in logical statements.
- Effective in Domains Based on Rules: Symbolic AI offers accurate and deterministic solutions in fields like business logic, law, and mathematics.

Nevertheless, symbolic AI faces challenges with:

- Learning from Data: It does not generalize well beyond predefined cases and necessitates a great deal of manual rule creation.
- Managing Unstructured Data: Without structured, predetermined knowledge, tasks like picture

recognition or natural language understanding are challenging.

- Scalability: As the number of rules increases, symbolic AI systems become complex and difficult to maintain.

Limitations of Subsymbolic AI

Neural networks and machine learning methods have gained prominence due to their ability to:

- Learn from Large Datasets: They can detect patterns in vast amounts of unstructured data, making them ideal for fields like image processing and natural language processing.
- Adapt and Improve Over Time: Neural networks adjust their parameters based on experience, making them flexible and capable of continuous learning.

Despite these advantages, subsymbolic AI faces significant drawbacks:

- Lack of Interpretability: Neural networks behave as black boxes, making it difficult to grasp how they arrive at judgments.

- Requirement for Large Datasets: Training deep learning models requires massive volumes of labeled data, which is not always available.

- Difficulties with Abstraction and Reasoning:** Neural networks are strong in pattern recognition but weak in logical inference and knowledge representation.

The Importance of Mixed AI

Hybrid AI combines the best features of both methods by combining subsymbolic learning and symbolic reasoning. This allows AI systems to:

- Combine Logical Reasoning with Pattern Recognition: Enabling AI to not only find patterns in data but also analyze and explain them.

- Improve Generalization and Adaptability: Making AI more robust across different domains without requiring enormous labeled datasets.

- Enhance Interpretability: By incorporating symbolic logic, hybrid AI systems can provide more transparent explanations for their decisions.

By merging these methodologies, hybrid AI offers a more balanced, efficient, and scalable approach to intelligent system development.

9.2 Neuro-Symbolic AI: Integrating Deep Learning with Logical Reasoning

The core of hybrid AI is neuro-symbolic integration, where deep learning models are combined with symbolic reasoning frameworks.

Neuro-Symbolic AI Methods

A number of strategies have been proposed to combine neural and symbolic methods:

- Symbolic Knowledge Injection: To enhance reasoning abilities, neural networks are trained using explicit logical rules.
- Knowledge Graph Augmented Learning: Structured knowledge from symbolic databases (such as knowledge graphs) is included into deep learning models.

- Neural-Symbolic Reinforcement Learning: AI agents use both subsymbolic pattern recognition and symbolic reasoning to develop the best decision-making rules.

The following are some examples of architectures:

1. Deep Neural Networks with Rule-Based Constraints

- Neural networks produce predictions that are verified by means of symbolic rules.
- Example: Neural-Symbolic Theorem Provers, where neural models predict logical inferences and symbolic systems verify correctness.

2. Knowledge Graph-Guided Neural Networks

- Networks use knowledge graphs to enhance data-driven learning.
- Example: IBM Watson, which mixes deep learning with symbolic knowledge databases for enhanced question-answering.

3. Hybrid AI in Language Processing

- Deep learning extracts patterns from text, while symbolic reasoning organizes responses.

- Example: AI chatbots, where symbolic approaches maintain consistency and deep learning enhances natural language understanding.

These techniques constitute the cornerstone of modern neuro-symbolic AI research, pushing the bounds of artificial intelligence beyond typical machine learning.

9.3 Applications of Hybrid AI: Self-Driving Cars, Healthcare, and More

Hybrid AI has already proved its utility in several areas, solving challenges that require both pattern recognition and logical reasoning.

1. Autonomous Vehicles

Both perception (subsymbolic AI) and decision-making (symbolic AI) are necessary for autonomous cars to navigate safely.

- Camera feeds are analyzed by deep learning models to identify objects, lanes, and traffic signals.
- Symbolic AI frameworks enforce decision-making

limitations and traffic regulations.

- By combining real-time sensor data with logical inference, hybrid planning algorithms provide safe and easy travel.

2. Medical diagnosis and healthcare

To help physicians, medical AI systems require explainable decision-making and data-driven pattern recognition.

- In order to identify abnormalities, neural networks examine medical pictures, such as MRIs and X-rays.
- Symbolic reasoning models guarantee that diagnoses adhere to accepted medical standards.
- Hybrid AI systems improve trust and dependability by offering interpretable treatment recommendations.

3. Identifying Fraud and Finance

To stop fraud, financial applications need logical validation and pattern detection.

- Neural networks are used to identify questionable transaction trends.

- Transactions are checked against fraud detection policies by symbolic rule-based systems.
- Hybrid AI solutions provide real-time fraud detection with explainable alerts.

4. Industrial Automation

Predictive analytics and automated planning are beneficial to supply chain management and manufacturing.

- Deep learning models predict demand and identify malfunctions in machinery.
- Symbolic AI schedulers optimize production planning and inventory control.
- Hybrid AI applications combine rule-based and predictive decision-making to increase efficiency.

As demonstrated by these applications, hybrid AI is bridging the gap between learning and reasoning to produce more dependable and smarter systems.

9.4 Obstacles and Prospects for Hybrid AI Research

Despite its promise, hybrid AI has a number of issues that

need to be resolved before it can be widely used.

Main Difficulties:

- Scalability: Combining neural and symbolic approaches makes computing more difficult.
- It is still challenging to guarantee consistency between learned patterns and symbolic logic in data-rule alignment.
- Generalization: Knowledge must be efficiently transferred between domains in hybrid models.
- "Explainability:" Although interpretability is enhanced by symbolic reasoning, hybrid models must maintain transparency without compromising functionality.

Future Directions

- Better Integration Frameworks: New algorithms and architectures are being developed to seamlessly combine deep learning with logical reasoning.
- Enhanced Knowledge Representation: Developments in semantic reasoning and knowledge graphs are assisting AI systems in comprehending and processing complex data more effectively.

- Neuro-Symbolic AI in General Intelligence: Hybrid AI is a vital step toward achieving **Artificial General Intelligence (AGI)** by enabling machines to think, reason, and learn more like humans.

As research continues, hybrid AI will redefine the future of artificial intelligence, creating more robust, adaptable, and interpretable systems across various industries.

A paradigm shift in artificial intelligence, hybrid AI combines the advantages of subsymbolic and symbolic approaches to produce more potent systems. Decision-making, generalization, and explainability are improved by hybrid AI, which combines logical reasoning with deep learning. Its transformative potential is demonstrated by its applications in autonomous systems, healthcare, finance, and industrial automation.

While challenges persist, ongoing research in neuro-symbolic AI is paving the way for more intelligent, scalable, and transparent AI systems that can reason, learn, and adapt. Next-generation artificial intelligence is probably going to be built on top of hybrid AI as this subject develops.

CHAPTER 10

SYMBOLIC AI'S FUTURE: REBIRTH AND DEVELOPMENT

In recent decades, there has been a significant change in the field of artificial intelligence (AI), with deep learning and neural networks taking center stage. Concerns about explainability, trustworthiness, and reasoning have, however, thrust symbolic AI back into the public eye as AI systems advance and are incorporated into vital fields like healthcare, finance, and law.

Researchers are working to create more interpretable, dependable, and morally aligned AI systems, which is leading to a revival of symbolic AI, which is focused on explicit logic, structured knowledge representations, and rule-based reasoning. The continuing significance of symbolic AI, its contributions to AI ethics, new developments in hybrid AI research, and its possible use in the quest for Artificial General Intelligence (AGI) are all covered in this chapter.

10.1 The Significance of Symbolic AI in the Deep Learning Era

Artificial intelligence has been transformed by deep learning and neural networks, which allow models to process natural language, identify patterns, and carry out intricate tasks with little assistance from humans. However, there are a number of drawbacks to these data-driven approaches that symbolic AI can assist with.

Deep Learning Drawbacks That Symbolic AI Can Solve
1. Lack of Explainability:

- Deep learning models function as "black boxes," making it challenging to comprehend how they make their decisions.

- To validate decisions in high-stakes domains like healthcare, finance, and law, explainability is essential.

- Symbolic AI enables transparent and interpretable AI judgments using rule-based reasoning and organized logic.

2. Data Inefficiency and Generalization Issues:

- Deep learning is ineffective for jobs with small datasets since it needs a lot of labeled data for training.
- Symbolic AI, on the other hand, uses pre-established rules and ontologies to reason with limited data.

3. Neural networks are excellent at identifying correlations, but they have trouble with causal reasoning and commonsense knowledge.

- AI systems can reason about cause and effect thanks to symbolic AI's ability to encode logical relationships and real-world facts.

4. Difficulties in Handling Abstract Knowledge:

- Deep learning by itself is unable to provide the semantic understanding needed for many AI applications.
- Symbolic AI offers organized representations of information through methods such as ontology-based reasoning and knowledge graphs.

The Transition to Hybrid AI

In light of these difficulties, hybrid AI approaches that blend symbolic reasoning and deep learning are becoming more and more popular among academics. By combining the structured logic and reasoning of symbolic AI with the pattern recognition capabilities of deep learning, this neuro-symbolic AI paradigm produces systems that are adaptive and interpretable.

10.2 Explainability and Credibility: The Advantages of Symbolic AI in AI Ethics

As AI is incorporated into important decision-making procedures, worries about ethical alignment, fairness, and bias have grown. Unique advantages in constructing ethical AI systems that are clear, reliable, and consistent with human ideals are provided by symbolic AI.

The Significance of Explainability in AI Ethics

1. Regulatory Compliance:

- Strict restrictions mandating AI-driven choices to be auditable and justifiable apply to industries including healthcare and finance.
- Organizations can trace and verify AI-generated

decisions thanks to symbolic AI's rule-based methodology.

2. Bias Detection and Mitigation:

- Biases typically come from the data used to train deep learning models.
- To guarantee that AI systems produce unbiased and equitable decisions, symbolic AI can embed ethical principles and fairness constraints.

3. Human-AI Collaboration:

- AI systems should function alongside humans in domains like business, law, and medicine, offering suggestions that users can comprehend and rely on.
- AI may justify its decisions using symbolic reasoning, which encourages human oversight and cooperation.

4. Preventing AI Misuse:

- Adversarial attacks, deepfake technologies, and AI-driven disinformation present moral dilemmas.
- The danger of AI-generated dishonesty can be decreased by using symbolic AI to enforce ethical

limits and discover anomalies.

In order to ensure that medical professionals understand and validate AI-generated suggestions, AI-driven diagnostic systems must offer clinicians interpretable insights. This is the case study for symbolic AI in healthcare ethics.

A hybrid AI system that combines symbolic reasoning and deep learning can explain diagnoses according to accepted medical guidelines and identify medical patterns (such as identifying tumors in X-rays).

Symbolic AI is essential to creating ethically acceptable AI systems by improving explainability, transparency, and trust.

10.3 New Developments: Neuro-Symbolic Computing, AI Alignment, and Other Trends

Aligning AI systems with human values, enhancing reasoning capabilities, and constructing hybrid models that combine the advantages of deep learning and symbolic techniques are the main goals of the next stage of AI research.

Important New Developments

- Making sure AI systems make choices that are consistent with human ethics, values, and social goals is the first goal of AI Alignment Research.
- AI models are being explicitly encoded with moral reasoning through the usage of symbolic AI.
- AI-powered legal frameworks that guarantee fair judicial decision-making are one example.

The combination of deep learning (for pattern recognition) and symbolic AI (for reasoning and logic) is known as Neuro-Symbolic AI.

- For instance, IBM Watson is combining neural networks and knowledge graphs to improve its question-answering capabilities.

3. Symbolic AI in Autonomous Systems

- For safety and compliance, self-driving automobiles and autonomous robotics need rule-based reasoning.
- Enhancing decision-making transparency, symbolic

AI makes sure AI-driven actions adhere to legal and ethical guidelines.

4. Enhanced Knowledge Representation Techniques

- AI is becoming more capable of organizing and processing information thanks to developments in knowledge graphs, semantic reasoning, and ontologies.
- For instance, Google's Knowledge Graph uses structured symbolic reasoning to improve search engine results.

In order to guarantee that AI systems are intelligent, ethical, and aligned with human values, symbolic AI will continue to shape the future of AI development as these trends progress.

10.4 Artificial General Intelligence (AGI) and the Function of Symbolic AI

The development of Artificial General Intelligence (AGI) , an AI system with human-like cognitive abilities that can reason, learn, and adapt across a variety of domains is the ultimate objective of AI research. Even though deep learning has made great strides, symbolic AI is crucial for obtaining AGI because of its capacity for knowledge representation and reasoning.

The Significance of Symbolic AI in AGI

1. Abstract and Logical Reasoning

- Beyond recognizing statistical patterns, AGI must understand, generalize, and reason about the world.
- The foundations of logic, deduction, and conceptual reasoning are supplied by symbolic AI.

Structured Knowledge Representation

- AGI necessitates a hierarchical, structured representation of knowledge like human cognition.
- Machines can process abstract concepts thanks to symbolic techniques like ontologies and rule-based reasoning.

3. Causal Understanding and Common Sense

- To get around the world, humans rely on cause-and-effect reasoning and common sense.

- These ideas are difficult for deep learning to grasp, but symbolic AI offers means for explicit causal reasoning.

4. Explainability and Trust

- To guarantee safe deployment, AGI needs to be understandable and controllable.
- AGI systems can justify decisions in human-readable formats thanks to symbolic AI.

The Hybrid Road to AGI

- AGI will probably be the result of a combination of neural networks and symbolic AI, using symbolic reasoning for higher-order cognition and deep learning for pattern recognition.
- In order to prepare the way for real AGI, hybrid AI architectures are being created to close the gap between structured reasoning and statistical learning.

The demand for explainable, ethical, and reasoning-capable AI systems is fueling a renaissance in symbolic AI. Even though deep learning has advanced AI, symbolic techniques are still essential for creating ethical, transparent, and intelligent AI solutions.

Symbolic AI will remain crucial in determining the direction of artificial intelligence as research into AI moves closer to hybrid AI models and AGI. For the next generation of intelligent systems, symbolic AI is not only important but also necessary due to logical reasoning, knowledge representation, and ethical AI alignment.

ABOUT THE AUTHOR

 Author and thought leader in the IT field Taylor Royce is well known. He has a two-decade career and is an expert at tech trend analysis and forecasting, which enables a wide audience to understand complicated concepts.

Royce's considerable involvement in the IT industry stemmed from his passion with technology, which he developed during his computer science studies. He has extensive knowledge of the industry because of his experience in both software development and strategic consulting.

Known for his research and lucidity, he has written multiple best-selling books and contributed to esteemed tech periodicals. Translations of Royce's books throughout the world demonstrate his impact.

Royce is a well-known authority on emerging technologies and their effects on society, frequently requested as a speaker at international conferences and as a guest on tech podcasts. He promotes the development of ethical technology, emphasizing problems like data privacy and the digital divide.

In addition, with a focus on sustainable industry growth, Royce mentors upcoming tech experts and supports IT education projects. Taylor Royce is well known for his ability to combine analytical thinking with technical know-how. He sees a time when technology will ethically benefit humanity.